Ninja Foodi Smart XL Grill Cookbook

The Popular and New Tasty Recipes for Indoor Grilling

and Air Frying（Beginners and Advanced Users）

Kimberly Corker

Table of Contents

Introduction

What is the Ninja Foodi Smart XL Grill?

The introduction of "Smart" technology in almost every domain and aspect of life has changed modern-day man's lifestyle. The cooking world has also been impacted vastly with the introduction of the Ninja Foodi Smart XL Grill. The reason is that it provides you with crucial cooking techniques like pressure cooking, grilling, air crisping, searing, broiling, sautéing, dehydrating, and grilling, etc. all in one single device. It is the reason why it is going to replace many conventional cooking appliances in your kitchen and provide you with a Smart, single solution to all your cooking modes. The best thing about the Ninja Foodi Smart

XL Grill is that it can be used both indoor as well as outdoor while being on camping or family picnics. Moreover, it is certified as a smoke-free device providing you with the most convenient possible.

The Ninja Foodi Smart XL Grill preserves the natural taste of the ingredients and gives a fresh aroma to your food. It helps you maintain the natural flavor, as well as the nutrition of the ingredients involved in the recipe of your food. Furthermore, it also comes with a kitchen thermometer, which is super beneficial in giving your food the right and most suitable cooking temperature. This correct temperature range is useful in giving your food the perfect and the right tenderness and crispiness. As a whole, the Ninja Foodi Smart XL Grill is considered to be one of the significant breakthroughs in the cooking world. It can be clearly referred to as the one ultimate choice for every single one of your cooking modes. The Ninja Foodi Smart XL Grill comes with various features and functions that make it stand ahead from the rest of its competitors.

The Features & Functions of Smart XL Grill

The main features of the Ninja Foodi Smart XL Grill are as follows:

- Easy to clean and is certified to be dishwasher safe.
- Smoke-free, and grilling capacity for approximately 7 oz. Burgers.
- Foodi™ Smart kitchen thermometer for accurate cooking temperature ranges.
- It can be used as an Air Fryer (4 quarters) too.
- Offers a Smart Cook System for customizing protein and doneness specifications.

The main functions of the Ninja Foodi Smart XL Grill are as follows:

BROIL, ROAST, BAKE, GRILL, AIR CRISP, DEHYDRATE, SAUTÉING, PRESSURE COOKING, SIMMERING.

Tips & Tricks for Cooking

Keep the following tips & tricks while using the Ninja Foodi Smart XL Grill to master it like a pro. These tricks and tips will yield you the ultimate and perfect results with every respective cooking mode. These include:

Steam

- Prefer steaming your veggies in the Cook & Crisp Basket. This will give them an extra and significant layer of texture. You can furthermore effectively toss them keenly with oil, followed by air crisping it with the help of the crisping lid. This will yield the ultimate taste and aroma.

Pressure

- To let your Ninja Foodi Smart XL Grill build pressure more efficiently, faster, and effectively, prefer using hot water while you are pressure cooking your food.

Air Crisp

- Place all your ingredients evenly inside the Cook & Crisp Basket so as to achieve the utmost perfection in browning your food. This will help you achieve a consistent as well as efficient browning of your ingredients.
- For achieving much better crispiness, you should thoroughly coat your veggies or other ingredients with a little quantity of oil before air crisping them. The final results will be very surprising and unmatched.

Broil

- For accomplishing an ultimately perfect touch of crispiness to your food, you can broil it as a secondary approach in an effective combo-cooking your foods with the perfect crispiness. We recommend performing a regular sneak and peek into your food throughout the course of the cooking time for having a better final result.

Sautéing and Searing

- For having a more efficient buildup of flavor in addition to thorough caramelization, we prefer searing your food thoroughly prior to cooking in the pressure cooking or the slow cooking mode.
- You can use the sauté or searing functions that can be utilized just like the stovetop. For simmering, use the LO function. For sautéing, use the MED function. And for boiling or searing different meats, use the HIGH function.
- We recommend keeping your meats at room temperature for around 20 to 30 minutes prior to searing them.
- You should also pat dry your meats before searing them. For better results, pat dry them before leaving them at room temperature prior to searing.

Bake & Roast

- We recommend using the Ninja Multi-purpose Pan instead of the regular baking pan for achieving perfect baking results with the Ninja Foodi Smart XL Grill.

Keep Warm

- You can utilize this function for preserving the original and natural taste, texture, and aroma of your cooked food by keeping it maintained at a food-safe temperature. It is better recommended for various ingredients that are thoroughly cooked in the Ninja Foodi Smart XL Grill, i.e., pulled pork, and dips, etc.

Dehydrate

- We recommend keeping your food as dry as possible prior to putting them inside the Cook & Crisp Basket.
- It is crucial to understand that almost all fruits & veggies will take approximately six to eight hours for dehydration. But, jerky will take five to seven hours to thoroughly dehydrate. Dehydration tenure is directly proportional to the crispiness of your food. The more crispiness you want, the more you should dehydrate your food.

- For having more space inside the basket, you can put all the veggies and fruits flat and closer, but you certainly cannot overlap them or even stack them together.

We recommend using the Roast function for around one minute at 300° Fahrenheit for effective pasteurization of the entire ingredients. We recommend preferring this function when you are using dehydrated fish and meats in the cooking recipe of your food.

Care & Cleaning Your Smart XL Grill

It might appear very tricky to thoroughly clean the Ninja Foodi Smart XL Grill, but it is not complicated at all. You merely need to follow certain easy steps, and your device is ready to go for another round. It is recommended to thoroughly clean the Ninja Foodi Smart XL Grill after every use. To clean the unit thoroughly and safely, follow the following guidelines:

- Let the device cool down before cleaning.
- Unplug the device from the power source.
- For quick cooling, keep the hood of the device open.
- The grill gate, splatter shield, crisper basket, cooking pot, cleaning brush, and the rest of the accessories are certified as **DISHWASHER SAFE**.
- The thermometer is not dishwasher safe.
- Rinse the accessories like splatter shield, grill gate, etc. for better cleaning results.
- Use the cleaning brush included with the device for handwashing.
- For cleaning baked-on cheese or sauces, utilize the other end of the cleaning brush for being used as a scrapper for effective hand washing.
- Either towel-dry or air-dry all the components after hand washing.
- **DO NOT** dip the main unit in any liquid, including water.
- **DO NOT** use any rasping cleaners or tools.

- **NEVER** use any sort of liquid cleaning solution near or on the thermometer.
- Always use a cotton swab or compressed air to avoid any damage to the jack.

In case of any grease or food residue left and stuck on the components of the Ninja Foodi Smart XL Grill, follow the following cleaning steps thoroughly:

1. If the residue is stuck on the splatter shield, grill gate, or any other accessory or part, soak it in warm soapy water solution before cleaning.

2. The splatter should be cleaned thoroughly after every use. For better cleansing, soak it in warm water overnight will assists efficiently in softening the stuck grease or sauces.

3. You can also deep clean the splatter shield by thoroughly immersing it in water and further boiling it for approximately 10 minutes.

4. Moreover, you can then rinse it effectively with room temperature water and let it dry properly for better results.

For deep cleaning the thermometer, you can soak both the silicone grip and the stainless steel tip in a container full of warm water. But, keep in mind that the jack or the cord **SHOULD NOT** be immersed or soaked in any solution, including water, as mentioned earlier. The thermometer holder of the Ninja Foodi Smart XL Grill is clearly **HANDWASH** only.

Chapter 1: Breakfast Recipes

Breakfast Frittata

Preparation Time: 10 minutes
Cooking Time: 10 minutes
Servings: 3

Ingredients:

- ¼ cup whole milk
- 2 eggs
- 3 tablespoons sugar
- 1/8 teaspoon vanilla extract
- 4 bread slices
- 2 teaspoons olive oil
- 1/8 teaspoon ground cinnamon

Preparation:

1. Select the "Grill" button on the Ninja Foodi Smart XL Grill and regulate the time for 10 minutes at Medium.
2. Mingle bacon, mushrooms, tomatoes, salt, and black pepper in a bowl.
3. Whip eggs with cheese in another bowl.
4. Place the bacon mixture in the Ninja Foodi when it displays "Add Food" and top with the eggs mixture.
5. Grill for 10 minutes, flipping once in between.
6. Dole out in a platter and serve warm.

Serving Suggestions: You can enjoy this Breakfast Frittata with the toasted bread slices.

Variation Tip: You can add tomatoes and parsley in the frittata.

Nutritional Information per Serving:

Calories: 219 | **Fat:** 14.3g|**Sat Fat:** 4.3g|**Carbohydrates:** 11.5g|

Fiber: 3.3g|**Sugar:** 2.9g|**Protein:** 14.2g

Cajun Sausages

Preparation Time: 5 minutes
Cooking Time: 20 minutes
Servings: 3

Ingredients:

- 1½ pounds ground sausage
- 1 teaspoon chili flakes
- 1 teaspoon dried thyme
- ½ teaspoon cayenne
- 1 teaspoon onion powder
- 3 teaspoons garlic, minced
- ½ teaspoon paprika
- 2 teaspoons brown sugar
- 2 teaspoons Tabasco
- Sea salt and black pepper, to taste

Preparation:

1. Select the "Grill" button on the Ninja Foodi Smart XL Grill and regulate the time for 20 minutes at Medium.
2. Mingle ground sausage with Tabasco sauce, spices, and herbs in a bowl.
3. Make sausage-shaped patties from this mixture.
4. Place the patties in the Ninja Foodi when it displays "Add Food".
5. Grill for 20 minutes, flipping once in between.
6. Dole out in a platter and serve warm.

Serving Suggestions: Serve these Cajun Sausages inside the buns.

Variation Tip: You can use pork, chicken, or beef sausages as required.

Nutritional Information per Serving:

Calories: 138|**Fat:** 9.7g|**Sat Fat:** 4.7g|**Carbohydrates:** 2.5g|
Fiber: 0.3g|**Sugar:** 0.9g|**Protein:** 10.3g

Bacon Bombs

Preparation Time: 5 minutes
Cooking Time: 7 minutes
Servings: 4

Ingredients:

- 3 large eggs, lightly beaten
- Cooking spray
- ounce cream cheese, softened
- 4-ounces whole-wheat pizza dough, freshly prepared
- 3 bacon slices, crisped and crumbled
- 1 tablespoon fresh chives, chopped

Preparation:

1. Select the "Bake" button on the Ninja Foodi Smart XL Grill and regulate the time for 16 minutes at 350 degrees F.
2. Break eggs in a non-stick pan and sauté for 1 minute.
3. Blend in the bacon, chives, and cream cheese and keep aside.
4. Split the pizza dough into 4 equal pieces and roll each piece into a circle.
5. Put ¼ of the egg mixture in the center of the dough circle and seal the edges with water.
6. Arrange the doughs in the Ninja Foodi when it displays "Add Food" and spray them with cooking oil.
7. Bake for 6 minutes and shift into a platter to serve warm.

Serving Suggestions: Feel free to top the Bacon Bombs with fresh herbs of your choice before serving.

Variation Tip: Pancetta can be used instead of bacon.

Nutritional Information per Serving:

Calories: 284|**Fat:** 7.9g|**Sat Fat:** 0g|**Carbohydrates:** 46g|
Fiber: 3.6g|**Sugar:** 5.5g|**Protein:** 7.9g

Swiss Cheese Sandwiches

Preparation Time: 5 minutes
Cooking Time: 18 minutes
Servings: 2

Ingredients:

- 2 slices sourdough bread
- 3 tablespoons half and half cream
- 1 egg
- 2-ounces deli turkey, sliced
- 2-ounces deli ham, sliced
- ¼ teaspoon vanilla extract
- 2½ ounces Swiss cheese, sliced
- 1 teaspoon butter, melted

Preparation:

1. Select the "Grill" button on the Ninja Foodi Smart XL Grill and regulate the time for 18 minutes at Medium.
2. Mingle the egg with vanilla extract and half and half cream in a bowl.
3. Top each bread slice with turkey and ham, followed by Swiss cheese slice.
4. Cover with the left over bread slices and slightly press.
5. Dip in the egg mixture and arrange them in the Ninja Foodi when it displays "Add Food".
6. Grill for 18 minutes, flipping once in between.
7. Dole out and serve warm.

Serving Suggestions: Serve topped with raspberry jam and powdered sugar.

Variation Tip: You can either use white or multigrain bread.

Nutritional Information per Serving:

Calories: 412**Fat:** 24.8g|**Sat Fat:** 12.4g|**Carbohydrates:** 43.8g|
Fiber: 3.9g|**Sugar:** 4.8g|**Protein:** 18.9g

Breakfast Pockets

Preparation Time: 5 minutes
Cooking Time: 11 minutes
Servings: 6

Ingredients:

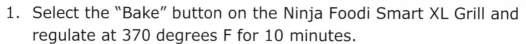

- 1 box puff pastry sheets
- ½ cup sausage crumbles, cooked
- ½ cup cheddar cheese, shredded
- 5 eggs
- ½ cup bacon, cooked

Preparation:

1. Select the "Bake" button on the Ninja Foodi Smart XL Grill and regulate at 370 degrees F for 10 minutes.
2. Break eggs in a non-stick pan and sauté for 1 minute.
3. Blend in the bacon and sausages and set aside.
4. Cut the puff pastry into equal-sized rectangles and add a scoop of cheese and egg mixture in the center.
5. Close the edges with water and shift into the Ninja Foodi when it displays "Add Food".
6. Bake for 10 minutes and dish out in a platter to serve warm.

Serving Suggestions: Fresh baby spring mix will be a great companion for these breakfast pockets.

Variation Tip: You can use any kind of fresh veggies for the filling of breakfast pockets.

Nutritional Information per Serving:

Calories: 387|**Fat:** 6g|**Sat Fat:** 9.9g|**Carbohydrates:** 41g|**Fiber:** 2.9g|**Sugar:** 5.2g|**Protein:** 6.6g

Sausage and Cheese Wraps

Preparation Time: 5 minutes
Cooking Time: 8 minutes
Servings: 4

Ingredients:

- 2 pieces of American cheese, cut into quarters
- 1 can of 8 counts crescent roll dough, refrigerated
- Ketchup, for dipping
- 8 heat n' serve sausages

Preparation:

1. Select the "Grill" button on the Ninja Foodi Smart XL Grill and regulate at Medium for 10 minutes.
2. Put the sausage and cheese over the crescent rolls.
3. Bind the sausages inside the rolls and seal the edges.
4. Arrange the rolls in the Ninja Foodi when it displays "Add Food".
5. Grill for 8 minutes, flipping once in between.
6. Dole out in a platter and serve warm.

Serving Suggestions: Enjoy your Sausage and Cheese Wraps with spicy salsa.

Variation Tip: You can also use Swiss cheese instead of American cheese.

Nutritional Information per Serving:

Calories: 331|**Fat:** 2.5g|**Sat Fat:** 0.5g|**Carbohydrates:** 69g|
Fiber: 12.2g|**Sugar:** 8.1g|**Protein:** 8.7g

Avocado Flautas

Preparation Time: 5 minutes
Cooking Time: 15 minutes
Servings: 4

Ingredients:

- ½ tablespoon butter
- 4 eggs, beaten
- ¼ teaspoon salt
- 4 fajita size tortillas
- ¼ cup feta cheese, crumbled
- ½ teaspoon chili powder
- ¼ cup Mexican cheese, shredded
- 1 teaspoon cumin
- 4 bacon slices, cooked
- 1/8 teaspoon pepper
- 2 oz cream cheese, softened

AVOCADO CRÈME

- ¼ teaspoon salt
- ¼ cup sour cream
- 1 small avocado
- 1/8 teaspoon black pepper
- ½ lime, juiced

Preparation:

1. Select the "Air Crisp" button on the Ninja Foodi Smart XL Grill and regulate at 400 degrees F for 10 minutes.
2. Put butter and eggs in a skillet on medium heat.
3. Sauté for 3 minutes and add salt, chili powder, pepper, and cumin.
4. Spread cream cheese on the tortillas and arrange bacon pieces on them.
5. Layer with egg mixture, followed by shredded cheese.

6. Firmly roll each tortilla and arrange them in the Ninja Foodi when it displays "Add Food".
7. Air crisp for 12 minutes, flipping once in between.
8. Put the ingredients of avocado crème in a blender and process until smooth.
9. Dole out the baked flautas in a platter and serve warm.

Serving Suggestions: It is best to serve with avocado cheese and cotija cheese.

Variation Tip: Use freshly shredded cheese.

Nutritional Information per Serving:

Calories: 212|**Fat:** 11.8g|**Sat Fat:** 2.2g|**Carbohydrates:** 14.6g| **Fiber:** 4.4g|**Sugar:** 3.2g|**Protein:** 17.3g

Scrambled Eggs

Preparation Time: 10 minutes
Cooking Time: 8 minutes
Servings: 4

Ingredients:

- 1 tablespoon milk
- 4 eggs
- 1 tablespoon olive oil
- Salt and black pepper, to taste

Preparation:

1. Select the "Grill" button on the Ninja Foodi Smart XL Grill and regulate the time for 8 minutes at Medium.
2. Whip eggs with milk, salt, and black pepper in a bowl.
3. Place the eggs mixture in the Ninja Foodi when it displays "Add Food" and shower with olive oil.
4. Grill for 8 minutes, flipping once in between.
5. Dole out in a platter and serve warm.

Serving Suggestions: Serve with toasted bagels.

Variation Tip: You can also use butter instead of olive oil.

Nutritional Information per Serving:

Calories: 151|**Fat:** 11.6g|**Sat Fat:** 4.6g|**Carbohydrates:** 0.7g|
Fiber: 0g|**Sugar:** 0.7g|**Protein:** 11.1g

Chapter 2: Snacks & Appetizer Recipes

Lemon Tofu

Preparation Time: 5 minutes
Cooking Time: 20 minutes
Servings: 2

Ingredients:

- 1 pound extra-firm tofu, drained, pressed, and cubed
- 1 tablespoon tamari
- 1 tablespoon arrowroot powder
- FOR THE SAUCE:
- 1 teaspoon lemon zest
- 1/3 cup lemon juice
- ½ cup water
- 2 tablespoons organic sugar
- 2 teaspoons arrowroot powder

Preparation:

1. Select the "Grill" button on the Ninja Foodi Smart XL Grill and regulate at Medium for 15 minutes.
2. Mingle the tofu, arrowroot powder, and tamari in a Ziploc bag.
3. Seal the Ziploc bag, shake it well, and marinate for about 1 hour.
4. Arrange the tofu in the Ninja Foodi when it displays "Add Food".
5. Stir well the tofu halfway through grilling and dole out in a plate when grilled completely.
6. Mingle all the ingredients for sauce in a skillet and cook for about 5 minutes on medium-low heat.
7. Place the tofu in the sauce and dish out to serve.

Serving Suggestions: Lemon Tofu can be served with Chinese Fried Rice.

Variation Tip: Lime can also be used instead of lemon.

Nutritional Information per Serving:

Calories: 338**Fat:** 3.8g|**Sat Fat:** 0.7g|**Carbohydrates:** 58.3g|
Fiber: 2.4g|**Sugar:** 20.2g|**Protein:** 5.4g

Grilled Vegetables

Preparation Time: 10 minutes
Cooking Time: 10 minutes
Servings: 3

Ingredients:

- 1½ tablespoons olive oil
- 1 pound asparagus, trimmed
- ½ pound cherry tomatoes, stemmed
- Salt and black pepper, to taste
- 1 zucchini, quartered lengthwise
- 1 corn ear, cut crosswise into 4 pieces
- 4 ounces cremini mushrooms, halved

FOR THE BASIL GARLIC SAUCE:

- ¼ cup olive oil
- 1¼ tablespoons red wine vinegar
- ½ teaspoon Dijon mustard
- Salt and black pepper, to taste
- 1½ tablespoons fresh parsley leaves, packed
- ¼ cup fresh basil leaves, packed
- 1 garlic clove, chopped

Preparation:

1. Select the "Grill" button on the Ninja Foodi Smart XL Grill and regulate at Medium for 20 minutes.
2. Put all the ingredients for basil garlic sauce in a food processor and process until smooth.
3. Season the asparagus, mushrooms, tomatoes, zucchini, and corn with salt and black pepper, and shower with olive oil.

4. Shift the vegetables in the Ninja Foodi when it displays "Add Food".
5. Dole out the tomatoes, mushrooms, and asparagus after 5 minutes and zuchhini and corn after 10 minutes.
6. Serve warm with basil garlic sauce.

Serving Suggestions: Serve these Grilled Vegetables as a side dish with steaks.

Variation Tip: You can also use garlic mayo sauce.

Nutritional Information per Serving:

Calories: 305|**Fat:** 23.6g|**Sat Fat:** 3.4g|**Carbohydrates:** 22.9g|
Fiber: 6.6g|**Sugar:** 8.6g|**Protein:** 7.6g

Spicy Cauliflower

Preparation Time: 5 minutes
Cooking Time: 20 minutes
Servings: 4

Ingredients:

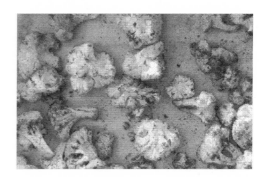

- 1 head cauliflower, cut into florets
- 1 tablespoon rice vinegar
- 1½ tablespoons tamari
- 3/4 cup onion white, thinly sliced
- 5 garlic cloves, finely sliced
- 1 tablespoon Sriracha
- ½ teaspoon coconut sugar
- 2 scallions, for garnish

Preparation:

1. Select the "Grill" button on the Ninja Foodi Smart XL Grill and regulate at Medium for 10 minutes.
2. Arrange the cauliflowers in the Ninja Foodi when it displays "Add Food".
3. Add the onions and garlic after 10 minutes and grill for 5 minutes.
4. Mingle soy sauce, sugar, salt, pepper, rice vinegar, and Sriracha in a bowl.
5. Drizzle the sugar mixture over the cauliflower and grill for 5 more minutes.
6. Dole out in a plate when grilled completely and garnish with scallions to serve.

Serving Suggestions: Serve the Spicy Cauliflower with marinara sauce or ranch dressing.

Variation Tip: You can use broccoli instead of cauliflower if desired.

Nutritional Information per Serving:

Calories: 378|**Fat:** 3.8g|**Sat Fat:** 0.7g|**Carbohydrates:** 13.3g| **Fiber:** 2.4g|**Sugar:** 5.2g|**Protein:** 5.4g

Italian Style Tofu

Preparation Time: 5 minutes
Cooking Time: 6 minutes
Servings: 2

Ingredients:

- ½ tablespoon tamari
- 4 ounces extra-firm tofu, pressed and cubed
- ½ tablespoon aquafaba
- 1/8 teaspoon dried basil
- ¼ teaspoon onion, granulated
- ¼ teaspoon dried oregano
- ¼ teaspoon garlic, granulated
- Black pepper, to taste

Preparation:

1. Select the "Air Crisp" button on the Ninja Foodi Smart XL Grill and regulate at 400 degrees F for 6 minutes.
2. Combine the tofu with all other ingredients in a bowl and marinate for around 30 minutes.
3. Arrange the tofu in the Ninja Foodi when it displays "Add Food".
4. Dole out the tofu when cooked completely and serve warm.

Serving Suggestions: Serve these Italian Style Tofu topped with parmesan cheese.

Variation Tip: You can also use soy sauce instead of tamari.

Nutritional Information per Serving:

Calories: 248|**Fat:** 2.4g|**Sat Fat:** 0.1g|**Carbohydrates:** 2.2g|
Fiber: 0.7g|**Sugar:** 0.8g|**Protein:** 44.3g

Crispy Artichoke Fries

Preparation Time: 5 minutes
Cooking Time: 12 minutes
Servings: 4

Ingredients:

- 1 (14 oz) can artichoke hearts, quartered

FOR THE DRY MIX:

- 1½ cups panko bread crumbs
- ½ teaspoon paprika
- ¼ teaspoon salt

FOR THE WET MIX:

- 1 cup all-purpose flour
- 1 cup almond milk
- ½ teaspoon garlic powder
- ¾ teaspoon salt
- ¼ teaspoon black pepper, or to taste

Preparation:

1. Select the "Air Crisp" button on the Ninja Foodi Smart XL Grill and regulate at 375 degrees F for 12 minutes.
2. Mingle all the dry ingredients in one bowl and wet ingredients in another bowl.
3. Coat the artichokes with the wet mixture and then dredge in the dry mixture.
4. Arrange the artichokes in the Ninja Foodi when it displays "Add Food".
5. Dole out the artichokes in a bowl and serve when air crisped completely.

Serving Suggestions: These Crispy Artichoke Fries will be great with any kind of dipping sauce.

Variation Tip: Strictly follow the ratio of ingredients.

Nutritional Information per Serving:

Calories: 341|**Fat:** 4g|**Sat Fat:** 0.5g|**Carbohydrates:** 36.4g| **Fiber:** 1.2g|**Sugar:** 12.4g|**Protein:** 10.3g

Corn Fritters

Preparation Time: 5 minutes
Cooking Time: 5 minutes
Servings: 4

Ingredients:

- 2 cups corn kernels, frozen
- 1/3 cup cornmeal, finely ground
- 1/3 cup flour
- ½ teaspoon baking powder
- 2 tablespoons green chiles with juices
- ½ teaspoon salt
- ¼ teaspoon paprika
- ¼ teaspoon black pepper
- Garlic powder, to taste
- Vegetable oil, for frying
- Onion powder, to taste
- ¼ cup Italian parsley, chopped

FOR THE TANGY DIPPING SAUCE:

- 4 tablespoons vegan mayonnaise
- 4 teaspoons Dijon mustard
- 2 teaspoons grainy mustard

Preparation:

1. Select the "Air Crisp" button on the Ninja Foodi Smart XL Grill and regulate the settings at 375 degrees F for 5 minutes.
2. Mingle seasonings, flour, baking powder, parsley, and cornmeal in a bowl.
3. Put 1 cup corn with salt, pepper, and 3 tablespoons almond milk in a food processor and process until smooth.
4. Merge the corn mixture with the flour mixture until well combined.

5. Fold in the remaining corn kernels and layer this mixture in a pan.
6. Lay the pan in the Ninja Foodi when it displays "Add Food".
7. Slice the corn fritters and dole out in a bowl.
8. Whip all the tangy dipping sauce ingredients in a bowl and serve with corn fritters.

Serving Suggestions: You can also serve the Corn Fritters with the ketchup.

Variation Tip: Potatoes can be replaced with corn to make potato fritters.

Nutritional Information per Serving:

Calories: 304|**Fat:** 30.6g|**Sat Fat:** 13.1g|**Carbohydrates:** 21.4g|
Fiber: 0.2g|**Sugar:** 9.5g|**Protein:** 4.6g

Crunchy Chicken

Preparation Time: 10 minutes
Cooking Time: 10 minutes
Servings: 2

Ingredients:

- 1 tablespoon olive oil
- 4 skinless, boneless chicken tenderloins
- 1 tablespoon Greek yogurt
- Salt and black pepper, to taste
- ½ teaspoon turmeric powder

Preparation:

1. Select the "Air Crisp" button on the Ninja Foodi Smart XL Grill and regulate the settings at 355 degrees F for 10 minutes.
2. Mingle yogurt with salt, black pepper and turmeric powder in a bowl.
3. Add the chicken tenderloins in the yogurt marinade and marinate for 30 minutes.
4. Arrange the chicken tenderloins in the Ninja Foodi when it displays "Add Food".
5. Dole out the chicken tenderloins in a platter and serve warm.

Serving Suggestions: Serving with mint dip enhances the taste of crunchy chicken.

Variation Tip: You can use low-fat yogurt if you are following low-fat diet.

Nutritional Information per Serving:

Calories: 394|**Fat:** 19.1g|**Sat Fat:** 4.5g|**Carbohydrates:** 0.2g|
Fiber: 0.1g|**Sugar:** 0.1g|**Protein:** 52.5g

Broccoli Bites

Preparation Time: 10 minutes
Cooking Time: 45 minutes
Servings: 3

Ingredients:

- 1/8 cup whole milk mozzarella cheese, grated
- 1 egg, beaten
- 1 cup broccoli florets
- Salt and black pepper, to taste
- 3/4 cups feta cheese, grated

Preparation:

1. Select the "Grill" button on the Ninja Foodi Smart XL Grill and regulate the settings at Medium for 15 minutes.
2. Pulse the broccoli with rest of the ingredients in a food processor until crumbled finely.
3. Roll this mixture into equal-sized balls and refrigerate for at least 30 minutes.
4. Arrange the balls in the Ninja Foodi when it displays "Add Food".
5. Dole out in a plate when grilled completely and serve warm.

Serving Suggestions: Sweet chili sauce will accompany these Broccoli Bites nicely.

Variation Tip: Feta cheese can be replaced with ricotta cheese too.

Nutritional Information per Serving:

Calories: 162|**Fat:** 12.4g|**Sat Fat:** 7.6g|**Carbohydrates:** 1.9g|**Fiber:** 0.5g|**Sugar:** 0.9g|**Protein:** 11.2g

Onion Rings

Preparation Time: 10 minutes
Cooking Time: 10 minutes
Servings: 2

Ingredients:

- 1 cup cream cheese
- 1 teaspoon baking powder
- 1 large onion, cut into ¼ inch slices and separated into rings
- 1 egg
- Salt, to taste

Preparation:

1. Select the "Air Crisp" button on the Ninja Foodi Smart XL Grill and regulate the settings at 360 degrees F for 10 minutes.
2. Mingle baking powder and salt in a bowl.
3. Whip egg with cream cheese in another bowl.
4. Immerse the onion rings in the egg mixture, then dredge into the dry mixture.
5. Arrange the onion rings in the Ninja Foodi when it displays "Add Food".
6. Dole out the onion rings in a platter and serve warm.

Serving Suggestions: Serve these Onion Rings with sour cream.

Variation Tip: You cam use breadcrumbs for enhanced crispiness.

Nutritional Information per Serving:

Calories: 266|**Fat:** 22.5g|**Sat Fat:** 13.4g|**Carbohydrates:** 9.9g|
Fiber: 1.7g|**Sugar:** 4.9g|**Protein:** 8g

Buffalo Chicken Wings

Preparation Time: 5 minutes
Cooking Time: 15 minutes
Servings: 3

Ingredients:

- 1 tablespoon olive oil
- ½ teaspoon garlic powder
- Salt and black pepper, to taste
- 6 chicken wings
- 1/4 cup red hot sauce

Preparation:

1. Select the "Grill" button on the Ninja Foodi Smart XL Grill and regulate the settings at Medium for 15 minutes.
2. Mingle the red hot sauce, garlic powder, salt, and black pepper in a bowl.
3. Dredge the chicken wings in this spice mixture and shower with the oil.
4. Arrange the chicken wings in the Ninja Foodi when it displays "Add Food".
5. Grill for 15 minutes, flipping once in between.
6. Dole out in a plate when grilled completely and serve warm.

Serving Suggestions: Serve these Buffalo Chicken Wings with marinara sauce.

Variation Tip: You can use fresh garlic too.

Nutritional Information per Serving:

Calories: 530|**Fat:** 37.9g|**Sat Fat:** 12.2g|**Carbohydrates:** 16.8g| **Fiber:** 0.5g|**Sugar:** 5.1g|**Protein:** 29.4g

Chapter 3: Vegetable & Sides Recipes

Salt and Vinegar Bok Choy

Preparation Time: 15 minutes
Cooking Time: 15 minutes
Servings: 6

Ingredients:

- 3 tablespoons canola oil
- 2 pounds bok choy, washed and dried
- 1 teaspoon ginger powder
- Coarse salt, to taste
- 3 tablespoons apple cider vinegar

Preparation:

1. Select the "Grill" button on the Ninja Foodi Smart XL Grill and regulate the settings at Medium for 15 minutes.
2. Mingle the bok choy, canola oil, ginger powder, apple cider vinegar, and salt in a bowl.
3. Rub the bok choy with hands for 2 minutes.
4. Arrange the bok choy in the Ninja Foodi when it displays "Add Food".
5. Grill for 15 minutes, turning once in between.
6. Dole out in a plate when grilled completely and serve warm.

Serving Suggestions: You can serve it as a side dish for any meat dish.

Variation Tip: Any kind of fresh mushrooms can be used.

Nutritional Information per Serving:

Calories: 82|**Fat:** 6.8g|**Sat Fat:** 0.8g|**Carbohydrates:** 3.6g|**Fiber:** 1.6g|**Sugar:** 1.8g|**Protein:** 2.3g

Miso-Glazed Brussels Sprouts

Preparation Time: 5 minutes
Cooking Time: 15 minutes
Servings: 2

Ingredients:

- 1½ teaspoons mirin
- 1 tablespoon sesame seeds
- ½ pound Brussels sprouts
- ¼ cup kimchi
- 2 teaspoons dark sesame oil
- 1½ tablespoons miso paste
- 1 tablespoon fresh basil, chopped

Preparation:

1. Select the "Roast" button on the Ninja Foodi Smart XL Grill and regulate the settings at Medium for 10 minutes.
2. Mingle the mirin, miso and 2 tablespoons water in a bowl.
3. Rub the Brussels sprouts with dark sesame oil with hands for 2 minutes.
4. Arrange the Brussels sprouts in the Ninja Foodi when it displays "Add Food".
5. Roast for about 10 minutes, tossing once in between.
6. Dole out in a plate when roasted completely and serve topped with mirin mixture.

Serving Suggestions: Serve with kimchi on the side.

Variation Tip: Make sure to cut the potato slices thinly.

Nutritional Information per Serving:

Calories: 149|**Fat:** 7.9g|**Sat Fat:** 1.2g|**Carbohydrates:** 16.8g|
Fiber: 5.5g|**Sugar:** 4.3g|**Protein:** 6.2g

Citrus Carrots

Preparation Time: 15 minutes
Cooking Time: 10 minutes
Servings: 4

Ingredients:

- 2 teaspoons fresh ginger, minced
- 2 teaspoons olive oil
- 3 cups carrots, peeled and sliced
- Salt and black pepper, to taste
- ½ cup fresh orange juice

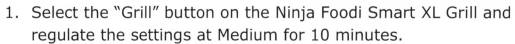

Preparation:

1. Select the "Grill" button on the Ninja Foodi Smart XL Grill and regulate the settings at Medium for 10 minutes.
2. Mingle the carrots with all other ingredients in a bowl.
3. Arrange the carrots in the Ninja Foodi when it displays "Add Food".
4. Grill for 10 minutes, stirring once in between.
5. Dole out in a plate when grilled completely and serve warm.

Serving Suggestions: Serve Citrus Carrots over a bed of rice.

Variation Tip: Make sure to use fresh carrots.

Nutritional Information per Serving:

Calories: 111|**Fat:** 6.6g|**Sat Fat:** 0.8g|**Carbohydrates:** 12g|
Fiber: 2.2g|**Sugar:** 6.7g|**Protein:** 1g

Grilled Cauliflower and Broccoli

Preparation Time: 10 minutes
Cooking Time: 10 minutes
Servings: 4

Ingredients:

- 3 tablespoons olive oil
- 1 head cauliflower, chopped into bite-size pieces
- ½ teaspoon salt
- 1 large avocado, sliced
- ½ cup vegetable broth
- ½ cup broccoli sprouts
- 1 tablespoon fresh lemon juice
- 3 garlic cloves, chopped
- 1 lemon zest

Preparation:

1. Select the "Grill" button on the Ninja Foodi Smart XL Grill and regulate the settings at Medium for 10 minutes.
2. Mingle the cauliflower and broccoli with all other ingredients in a bowl.
3. Arrange the cauliflower and broccoli mixture in the Ninja Foodi when it displays "Add Food".
4. Grill for 10 minutes, stirring once in between.
5. Dole out in a plate when grilled completely and serve warm.

Serving Suggestions: Serve Grilled Cauliflower and Broccoli over quinoa.

Variation Tip: You can also use carrots instead of broccoli.

Nutritional Information per Serving:

Calories: 226|**Fat:** 19.9g|**Sat Fat:** 3.3g|**Carbohydrates:** 10.9g|
Fiber: 5.8g|**Sugar:** 2.6g|**Protein:** 3.5g

Roasted Tomatoes

Preparation Time: 10 minutes
Cooking Time: 10 minutes
Servings: 3

Ingredients:

- 1 tablespoon onion, chopped finely
- 3 large tomatoes, halved
- ½ jalapeño pepper, seeded and minced
- Black pepper, to taste
- Salt, to taste
- ½ tablespoon fresh rosemary, minced
- 1 tablespoon olive oil
- ½ teaspoon fresh thyme, minced
- 2 cups fresh baby spinach
- 2 garlic cloves, minced
- ½ teaspoon fresh oregano, minced

Preparation:

1. Select the "Roast" button on the Ninja Foodi Smart XL Grill and regulate the settings at Medium for 10 minutes.
2. Season the tomatoes with salt and keep aside for about 1 hour.
3. Mingle the onion, garlic, jalapeño pepper, herbs and black pepper in a bowl.
4. Position the cut side up tomatoes in the Ninja Foodi when it displays "Add Food".
5. Pour the herb mixture over the tomatoes and shower with oil.
6. Roast for about 10 minutes, tossing once in between.
7. Dole out in a plate when roasted completely and serve warm.

Serving Suggestions: Enjoy these Roasted Tomatoes with yogurt dip.

Variation Tip: You can add spices of your choice in these veggie kabobs

Nutritional Information per Serving:

Calories: 85|**Fat:** 4.9g|**Sat Fat:** 0.6g|**Carbohydrates:** 9.4g|
Fiber: 3.2g|**Sugar:** 5.1g|**Protein:** 2.4g

Mediterranean Spinach With Cheese

Preparation Time: 10 minutes
Cooking Time: 15 minutes
Servings: 3

Ingredients:

- 2 tablespoons olive oil
- 3/4 cup feta cheese, grated
- Salt and black pepper, to taste
- 1 pound spinach, chopped and boiled
- 2 teaspoons fresh lemon zest, grated

Preparation:

1. Select the "Grill" button on the Ninja Foodi Smart XL Grill and regulate the settings at Medium for 15 minutes.
2. Mingle the spinach, olive oil, salt, and black pepper in a bowl.
3. Place the spinach mixture in the Ninja Foodi when it displays "Add Food".
4. Grill for 15 minutes, stirring once in between.
5. Dole out in a plate when grilled completely and top with lemon zest and cheese to serve.

Serving Suggestions: Serve with the topping of Kalamata Olives.

Variation Tip: You can also replace feta cheese with cottage cheese.

Nutritional Information per Serving:

Calories: 247|**Fat:** 18.7g|**Sat Fat:** 3.3g|**Carbohydrates:** 7.2g|
Fiber: 9.9g|**Sugar:** 2.3g|**Protein:** 9.9g

Cheesy Veggies

Preparation Time: 10 minutes
Cooking Time: 20 minutes
Servings: 3

Ingredients:

- 1 teaspoon canola oil
- 1 tomato, thinly sliced
- 1 teaspoon mixed dried herbs
- 1 zucchini, sliced
- Salt and black pepper, to taste
- 1 onion, thinly sliced
- 1 cup whole milk mozzarella cheese, grated

Preparation:

1. Select the "Bake" button on the Ninja Foodi Smart XL Grill and regulate the settings at 400 degrees F for 30 minutes.
2. Arrange the vegetables in the Ninja Foodi when it displays "Add Food".
3. Shower with canola oil and add mixed dried herbs, salt, and black pepper.
4. Layer with cheese and bake for about 30 minutes.
5. Dole out the cheesy vegetables when baked completely and serve warm.

Serving Suggestions: You can use these cheesy veggies along side the pasta.

Variation Tip: Cauliflower and broccoli can also be used as veggies.

Nutritional Information per Serving:

Calories: 305|**Fat:** 22.3g|**Sat Fat:** 13.2g|**Carbohydrates:** 8.3g| **Fiber:** 2.9g|**Sugar:** 4.2g|**Protein:** 15.2g

Bacon Bok Choy

Preparation Time: 10 minutes
Cooking Time: 15 minutes
Servings: 3

Ingredients:

- 2 tablespoons olive oil
- 4 bok choy, sliced
- Black pepper, to taste
- 2 bacon slices
- ½ cup Pecorino Romano cheese, grated
- 2 tablespoons fresh parsley, chopped
- 4 tablespoons coconut cream

Preparation:

1. Select the "Grill" button on the Ninja Foodi Smart XL Grill and regulate the settings at Medium for 15 minutes.
2. Mingle the bok choy with olive oil, coconut cream, parsley, salt, and black pepper in a bowl.
3. Arrange the bok choy mixture in the Ninja Foodi when it displays "Add Food".
4. Layer with bacon, followed by Pecorino Romano cheese.
5. Grill for 15 minutes and dole out when grilled completely.
6. Dole out in a plate when grilled completely and serve warm.

Serving Suggestions: Serve with the garnishing of pine nuts.

Variation Tip: You can use fresh basil instead of garlic powder.

Nutritional Information per Serving:

Calories: 112|**Fat:** 4.9g|**Sat Fat:** 1.9g|**Carbohydrates:** 1.9g|**Fiber:** 0.4g|**Sugar:** 0.8g|**Protein:** 3g

Ham Spinach Muffins

Preparation Time: 10 minutes
Cooking Time: 23 minutes
Servings: 3

Ingredients:

- 1 tablespoon olive oil
- 14-ounce ham, sliced
- 1 tablespoon unsalted butter, melted
- 1½ pounds fresh baby spinach
- 8 teaspoons coconut cream
- Salt and black pepper, to taste

Preparation:

1. Select the "Bake" button on the Ninja Foodi Smart XL Grill and regulate the settings at 355 degrees F for 20 minutes.
2. Cook the olive oil and spinach on medium heat for about 3 minutes.
3. Drain the liquid from the spinach completely.
4. Grease 4 ramekins with butter and layer the spinach in them, followed by ham slices.
5. Top with cream and season with salt and black pepper.
6. Arrange the ramekins in the Ninja Foodi when it displays "Add Food".
7. Layer with cheese and bake for about 20 minutes.
8. Dole out the muffins when baked completely and serve warm.

Serving Suggestions: Serve with your favourite sauce.

Variation Tip: You can also use bacon or sausages instead of ham.

Nutritional Information per Serving:

Calories: 188|**Fat:** 12.5g|**Sat Fat:** 4.4g|**Carbohydrates:** 4.9g|
Fiber: 2g|**Sugar:** 0.3g|**Protein:** 14.6g

Chapter 4: Fish & Seafood Recipes

Air Crisped Salmon

Preparation Time: 5 minutes
Cooking Time: 8 minutes
Servings: 2

Ingredients:

- 4 teaspoons avocado oil
- 2 salmon fillets
- 4 teaspoons paprika
- Lemon wedges
- Salt and coarse black pepper, to taste

Preparation:

1. Choose the "Air Crisp" button on the Ninja Foodi Smart XL Grill and regulate the settings at 390 degrees F for 8 minutes.
2. Brush the salmon fillets with avocado oil, salt, black pepper, and paprika.
3. Arrange the salmon fillets in the Ninja Foodi when it displays "Add Food".
4. Air crisp for about 8 minutes, tossing the fillets in between.
5. Dole out the fillets in a platter and serve warm.

Serving Suggestions: Enjoy with roasted parsnip puree.

Variation Tip: Salmon should look bright and shiny.

Nutritional Information per Serving:

Calories: 308|**Fat:** 20.5g|**Sat Fat:** 3g|**Carbohydrates:** 10.3g|
Fiber: 4.3g|**Sugar:** 5.5g|**Protein:** 49g

4 Ingredients Catfish

Preparation Time: 5 minutes
Cooking Time: 12 minutes
Servings: 4

Ingredients:

- 1 tablespoon parsley, chopped
- ¼ cup Louisiana fish seasoning
- 4 catfish fillets
- 1 tablespoon olive oil

Preparation:

1. Select the "Grill" button on the Ninja Foodi Smart XL Grill and regulate the settimgs at Medium for 12 minutes.
2. Mingle the catfish fillets with Louisiana fish seasoning in a bowl.
3. Arrange the fillets in the Ninja Foodi when it displays "Add Food" and shower with olive oil.
4. Grill for about 12 minutes, tossing the fillets in between.
5. Dole out the fillets in a platter and garnish with parsley to serve.

Serving Suggestions: Serve with steamed asparagus.

Variation Tip: For best result, use freshly squeezed lime juice.

Nutritional Information per Serving:

Calories: 253|**Fat:** 7.5g|**Sat Fat:** 1.1g|**Carbohydrates:** 10.4g|
Fiber: 0g|**Sugar:** 4.4g|**Protein:** 13.1g

Broiled Tilapia

Preparation Time: 5 minutes
Cooking Time: 8 minutes
Servings: 2

Ingredients:

- Old Bay seasoning, to taste
- 1 pound tilapia fillets
- Lemon pepper, to taste
- Molly mcbutter, to taste
- Salt, to taste
- Cooking oil spray

Preparation:

1. Select the "Broil" button on the Ninja Foodi Smart XL Grill and regulate the settings for 8 minutes.
2. Brush the tilapia fillets with all the seasonings.
3. Arrange the tilapia fillets in the Ninja Foodi when it displays "Add Food" and shower with cooking oil spray.
4. Broil for about 8 minutes, tossing the fillets in between.
5. Dole out the fillets in a platter and serve warm.

Serving Suggestions: Serve the broiled tilapia with fresh baby greens.

Variation Tip: Cod can also be replaced with tilapia.

Nutritional Information per Serving:

Calories: 192|**Fat:** 2.3g|**Sat Fat:** 1g|**Carbohydrates:** 0.5g|
Fiber: 0g|**Sugar:** 0g|**Protein:** 42.2g

Breaded Shrimp

Preparation Time: 5 minutes
Cooking Time: 16 minutes
Servings: 4

Ingredients:

- 1 pound shrimp, peeled and deveined
- 2 eggs
- ½ cup panko breadcrumbs
- 1 teaspoon garlic powder
- 1 teaspoon black pepper
- 1 teaspoon ginger
- ½ cup onion, peeled and diced

Preparation:

1. Select the "Air Crisp" button on the Ninja Foodi Smart XL Grill and regulate the settings at 350 degrees F for 16 minutes.
2. Mingle breadcrumbs, spices, and onions in one bowl, and whip eggs in another bowl.
3. Dip the shrimp in the whipped eggs and then dredge in the breadcrumbs mixture.
4. Arrange the shrimp in the Ninja Foodi when it displays "Add Food".
5. Grill for about 16 minutes, tossing the shrimps in between.
6. Dole out the shrimps in a platter and serve warm.

Serving Suggestions: Serve breaded shrimp with lemon butter.

Variation Tip: You can also use fresh ginger and garlic instead of powdered ginger and garlic.

Nutritional Information per Serving:

Calories: 212|**Fat:** 4.4g|**Sat Fat:** 1.3g|**Carbohydrates:** 11.9g|
Fiber: 1.6g|**Sugar:** 1.2g|**Protein:** 30g

Southern Catfish

Preparation Time: 5 minutes
Cooking Time: 13 minutes
Servings: 4

Ingredients:

- 1 lemon
- 2 pounds catfish fillets
- 1 cup milk
- ½ cup yellow mustard

CORNMEAL SEASONING MIX:

- 2 tablespoons dried parsley flakes
- ½ cup cornmeal
- ¼ cup all-purpose flour
- ¼ teaspoon chili powder
- ¼ teaspoon black pepper
- ¼ teaspoon cayenne pepper
- ½ teaspoon kosher salt
- ¼ teaspoon onion powder
- ¼ teaspoon garlic powder

Preparation:

1. Select the "Air Crisp" button on the Ninja Foodi Smart XL Grill and regulate the settings at 400 degrees F for 13 minutes.
2. Mingle the Catfish with milk and lemon juice and let it refrigerate for about 30 minutes.
3. Toss well the cornmeal seasoning ingredients in a bowl.
4. Pat dry the catfish fillets and scrub with mustard.
5. Coat the catfish fillets with cornmeal mixture and arrange the fillets in the Ninja Foodi when it displays "Add Food".
6. Shower with cooking oil and air crisp for about 10 minutes, tossing the fillets in between.

7. Dole out the fillets in a platter and serve warm.

Serving Suggestions: Quinoa salad will be a great choice for serving.

Variation Tip: Season the fish according to your choice.

Nutritional Information per Serving:

Calories: 231|**Fat:** 20.1g|**Sat Fat:** 2.4g|**Carbohydrates:** 20.1g|

Fiber: 0.9g|**Sugar:** 3.6g|**Protein:** 14.6g

Tuna Patties

Preparation Time: 5 minutes
Cooking Time: 10 minutes
Servings: 4

Ingredients:

- 2 cans tuna, packed in water
- 1½ tablespoons almond flour
- 1½ tablespoons mayonnaise
- Pinch of salt and pepper
- ½ teaspoon onion powder
- 1 teaspoon garlic powder
- 1 teaspoon dried dill
- ½ lemon, juiced

Preparation:

1. Select the "Grill" button on the Ninja Foodi Smart XL Grill and regulate the settings at Medium for 10 minutes.
2. Mingle all the tuna patties ingredients in a bowl and create equal-sized patties from this mixture.
3. Arrange the tuna patties in the Ninja Foodi when it displays "Add Food".
4. Grill for about 10 minutes, tossing the patties once in between.
5. Dole out the fillets in a platter and serve warm.

Serving Suggestions: Serve with the garlic mayo dip.

Variation Tip: You can also use fresh garlic instead of powdered garlic.

Nutritional Information per Serving:

Calories: 338|**Fat:** 3.8g|**Sat Fat:** 0.7g|**Carbohydrates:** 8.3g|

Fiber: 2.4g|**Sugar:** 3g|**Protein:** 15.4g

Chili Lime Tilapia

Preparation Time: 5 minutes
Cooking Time: 10 minutes
Servings: 2

Ingredients:

- 1 pound tilapia fillets
- 1 cup panko crumbs
- ½ cup flour
- Salt and black pepper, to taste
- 1 lime, juiced
- 1 tablespoon chili powder
- 2 eggs

Preparation:

1. Select the "Grill" button on the Ninja Foodi Smart XL Grill and regulate the settings at Medium for 10 minutes.
2. Mingle the crumbs with salt, chili powder, and black pepper in a bowl.
3. Place flour in one bowl and whip egg in another bowl.
4. Dredge the fillets in the flour, then dip in the egg.
5. Cover with the panko mixture and arrange the fillets in the Ninja Foodi when it displays "Add Food".
6. Grill for about 10 minutes, tossing the fillets once in between.
7. Dole out the fillets in a platter and shower with lime juice to serve.

Serving Suggestions: Roasted potatoes make a great side for Chili Lime Tilapia.

Variation Tip: If you want a gluten-free option, then use pork rinds instead of breadcrumbs.

Nutritional Information per Serving:

Calories: 327|**Fat:** 3.5g|**Sat Fat:** 0.5g|**Carbohydrates:** 33.6g|
Fiber: 0.4g|**Sugar:** 9.2g|**Protein:** 24.5g

Shrimp Lettuce Wraps

Preparation Time: 20 minutes
Cooking Time: 10 minutes
Servings: 10

Ingredients:

- 2 tablespoons extra-virgin olive oil
- 1 pound shrimps
- 2 garlic cloves, minced
- ½ cup summer squash, chopped
- 1 onion, chopped
- ½ cup zucchini, chopped
- Black pepper, to taste
- 1 green bell pepper, seeded and chopped
- ½ teaspoon curry powder
- 1 cup carrot, peeled and chopped
- 2 tablespoons low-sodium soy sauce
- 10 large lettuce leaves

Preparation:

1. Select the "Grill" button on the Ninja Foodi Smart XL Grill and regulate the settings at Medium for 10 minutes.
2. Mingle the shrimps with soy sauce, curry powder, vegetables, and black pepper in a bowl.
3. Arrange the shrimps mixture in the Ninja Foodi when it displays "Add Food".
4. Grill for about 10 minutes and dole out the shrimps mixture.
5. Insert the shrimp mixture over the lettuce leaves and serve.

Serving Suggestions: Enjoy the Shrimp Lettuce Wraps with grilled vegetables.

Variation Tip: You can also use mirin insteag of soy sauce.

Nutritional Information per Serving:

Calories: 97|**Fat:** 3.7g|**Sat Fat:** 0.6g|**Carbohydrates:** 5.1g|
Fiber: 0.9g|**Sugar:** 2.3g|**Protein:** 11.1g

Salmon and Broccoli

Preparation Time: 15 minutes
Cooking Time: 10 minutes
Servings: 5

Ingredients:

- 2 garlic cloves, minced
- 1 pound salmon, chunked
- 1 tablespoon coconut aminos, gluten free
- 5 cups broccoli, chopped
- 3 scallions, thinly sliced
- 3 tablespoons olive oil
- 1 tablespoon dark sesame oil
- ¾ teaspoon red pepper flakes
- inch piece fresh ginger, minced
- Salt and black pepper, to taste

Preparation:

1. Select the "Grill" button on the Ninja Foodi Smart XL Grill and regulate the settings at Medium for 10 minutes.
2. Mingle the salmon chunks and broccoli with rest of the ingredients in a bowl.
3. Arrange the salmon mixture in the Ninja Foodi when it displays "Add Food".
4. Grill for about 10 minutes and dole out to serve warm.

Serving Suggestions: Serve topped with sesame seeds.

Variation Tip: You can also use cauliflower instead of broccoli.

Nutritional Information per Serving:

Calories: 276|**Fat:** 18.3g|**Sat Fat:** 2.4g|**Carbohydrates:** 8.7g|

Fiber: 3.1g|**Sugar:** 1.8g|**Protein:** 21.1g

Paprika Shrimp

Preparation Time: 10 minutes
Cooking Time: 15 minutes
Servings: 3

Ingredients:

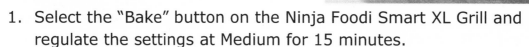

- Salt, to taste
- ½ teaspoon smoked paprika
- 2 tablespoons avocado oil
- 1 pound tiger shrimp

Preparation:

1. Select the "Bake" button on the Ninja Foodi Smart XL Grill and regulate the settings at Medium for 15 minutes.
2. Mingle the tiger shrimp, avocado oil, salt, and paprika in a bowl.
3. Arrange the shrimp mixture in the Ninja Foodi when it displays "Add Food".
4. Bake for about 10 minutes and dole out to serve warm.

Serving Suggestions: You can also serve topped with cayenne pepper.

Variation Tip: Avoid shrimp that smell like ammonia.

Nutritional Information per Serving:

Calories: 173|**Fat:** 8.3g|**Sat Fat:** 1.3g|**Carbohydrates:** 0.1g|
Fiber: 0.1g|**Sugar:** 0g|**Protein:** 23.8g

Chapter 5: Poultry Recipes

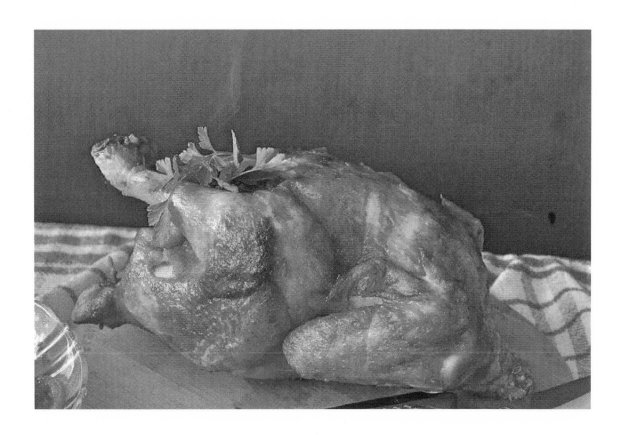

Southern-Style Chicken

Preparation Time: 5 minutes
Cooking Time: 20 minutes
Servings: 6

Ingredients:

- 2 cups Ritz crackers, crushed
- 1 tablespoon fresh parsley, minced
- 1 teaspoon garlic salt
- ¼ teaspoon rubbed sage
- 1 teaspoon paprika
- 1 large egg, beaten
- ½ teaspoon black pepper
- 1 (3-4 pounds) broiler/fryer chicken, cut up
- ¼ teaspoon ground cumin

Preparation:

1. Select the "Air Crisp" button on the Ninja Foodi Smart XL Grill and regulate the settings at 350 degrees F for 20 minutes.
2. Whip egg in a bowl and mingle rest of the ingredients except chicken in another bowl.
3. Immerse the chicken in the whipped egg and then dredge in the dry mixture.
4. Arrange the chicken in the Ninja Foodi when it displays "Add Food".
5. Air crisp for about 20 minutes and dole out to serve warm.

Serving Suggestions: Serve with dinner rolls.

Variation Tip: Fresh coriander can also be used instead of parsley.

Nutritional Information per Serving:

Calories: 391|**Fat:** 2.8g|**Sat Fat:** 0.6g|**Carbohydrates:** 16.5g|
Fiber: 9.2g|**Sugar:** 4.2g|**Protein:** 26.6g

Herbed Roasted Chicken

Preparation Time: 5 minutes
Cooking Time: 18 minutes
Servings: 4

Ingredients:

- Salt, to taste
- 4 chicken thighs, skin on, bone removed
- Black pepper, for garnish
- Garlic powder, to taste

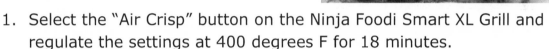

Preparation:

1. Select the "Air Crisp" button on the Ninja Foodi Smart XL Grill and regulate the settings at 400 degrees F for 18 minutes.
2. Dust the chicken with garlic powder and salt.
3. Arrange the chicken in the Ninja Foodi when it displays "Add Food".
4. Air crisp for 18 minutes, flipping once in between.
5. Dole out in a platter and dust with black pepper to serve.

Serving Suggestions: Roasted vegetables will accompany this roasted chicken nicely.

Variation Tip: Rub the chicken with your hands for even coating.

Nutritional Information per Serving:

Calories: 140|**Fat:** 7.9g|**Sat Fat:** 1.8g|**Carbohydrates:** 2.6g|
Fiber: 1.8g|**Sugar:** 1.5g|**Protein:** 7.2g

Sesame Chicken Breast

Preparation Time: 5 minutes
Cooking Time: 20 minutes
Servings: 2

Ingredients:

- 2 chicken breasts
- 2 tablespoons sesame oil
- 1 teaspoon kosher salt
- ¼ teaspoon cayenne pepper
- 1 tablespoon sweet paprika
- ½ teaspoon black pepper
- 1 tablespoon onions powder
- 1 tablespoon garlic powder

Preparation:

1. Press the "Bake" button on the Ninja Foodi Smart XL Grill and adjust the time for 20 minutes at 380 degrees F.
2. Season the chicken breasts with sesame oil and all other spices.
3. Place the chicken in the Ninja Foodi when it shows "Add Food".
4. Bake for 20 minutes and dole out to serve warm.

Serving Suggestions: Serve with cheesy baked asparagus.

Variation Tip: Don't accept any chicken breasts that are soft and discolored.

Nutritional Information per Serving:

Calories: 453|**Fat:** 2.4g|**Sat Fat:** 3g|**Carbohydrates:** 18g|
Fiber: 2.3g|**Sugar:** 3.3g|**Protein:** 23.2g

Crispy Chicken and Potatoes

Preparation Time: 5 minutes
Cooking Time: 15 minutes
Servings: 4

Ingredients:

- 15 oz can potatoes, drained
- 1 teaspoon olive oil
- 1 teaspoon Lawry's seasoned salt
- 3/8 cup cheddar cheese, shredded
- ¼ teaspoon paprika
- 8 oz chicken breast, boneless, skinless, and cubed
- 1/8 teaspoon black pepper
- 4 bacon slices, cooked and cut into strips

Preparation:

1. Select the "Broil" button on the Ninja Foodi Smart XL Grill and regulate the settiings for 20 minutes.
2. Scrub the chicken and potato pieces with spices and olive oil.
3. Arrange the chicken and potatoes in the Ninja Foodi when it displays "Add Food".
4. Put the bacon and cheese on the top and start broiling, flipping once in between.
5. Dole out in a platter and top with dried herbs to serve.

Serving Suggestions: Serve with yogurt mint dip.

Variation Tip: You can increase the spices according to your taste.

Nutritional Information per Serving:

Calories: 301|**Fat:** 15.8g|**Sat Fat:** 2.7g|**Carbohydrates:** 31.7g|**Fiber:** 0.3g|**Sugar:** 6.1g|**Protein:** 28.2g

Lemon Pepper Chicken

Preparation Time: 5 minutes
Cooking Time: 20 minutes
Servings: 4

Ingredients:

- 4 boneless-skinless chicken breasts
- 1 tablespoon lemon pepper
- 1 teaspoon table salt
- 1½ teaspoons granulated garlic

Preparation:

1. Select the "Grill" button on the Ninja Foodi Smart XL Grill and regulate the settings at Medium for 20 minutes.
2. Dust the chicken breasts with salt, garlic, and lemon pepper.
3. Arrange the chicken in the Ninja Foodi when it displays "Add Food".
4. Grill for about 20 minutes, flipping once in between.
5. Dole out in a platter and serve warm.

Serving Suggestions: You can serve this Lemon Pepper Chicken with quinoa..

Variation Tip: You can use some fresh lemons too.

Nutritional Information per Serving:

Calories: 284|**Fat:** 25g|**Sat Fat:** 1g|**Carbohydrates:** 35g|
Fiber: 2g|**Sugar:** 5.5g|**Protein:** 26g

Herb-Marinated Thighs

Preparation Time: 5 minutes
Cooking Time: 18 minutes
Servings: 6

Ingredients:

- ¼ cup olive oil
- 2 teaspoons lemon juice
- 2 teaspoons garlic powder
- 6 chicken thighs, bone-in, skin-on
- ½ teaspoon dried sage
- 1 teaspoon spike seasoning
- ½ teaspoon onion powder
- 1 teaspoon dried basil
- ½ teaspoon dried oregano
- ¼ teaspoon black pepper

Preparation:

1. Select the "Roast" button on the Ninja Foodi Smart XL Grill and regulate the settings for 18 minutes.
2. Mingle the chicken thighs with olive oil, lemon juice, oregano, basil, garlic powder, spike seasoning, onion powder, sage, and black pepper in a bowl.
3. Toss thoroughly and refrigerate to marinate for about 5 hours.
4. Place the chicken thighs in the Ninja Foodi when it displays "Add Food".
5. Roast for about 18 minutes, flipping once in between.
6. Dole out in a platter and serve warm.

Serving Suggestions: Mashed potatoes will go great with these herb-marinated thighs.

Variation Tip: Butter can replace olive oil in this recipe.

Nutritional Information per Serving:

Calories: 338|**Fat:** 8g|**Sat Fat:** 1g|**Carbohydrates:** 8g|
Fiber: 1g|**Sugar:** 3g|**Protein:** 13g

Chicken Broccoli

Preparation Time: 5 minutes
Cooking Time: 20 minutes
Servings: 4

Ingredients:

- 1 pound chicken breast, boneless and cut into bite-sized pieces
- 1 tablespoon soy sauce, low sodium
- 1 tablespoon olive oil
- ½ pound broccoli, cut into small florets
- 2 teaspoons hot sauce
- ½ onion, sliced
- 1 teaspoon sesame seed oil
- Salt, to taste
- Black pepper, to taste
- ½ teaspoon garlic powder
- 1 tablespoon fresh minced ginger
- 2 teaspoons rice vinegar

Preparation:

1. Select the "Grill" button on the Ninja Foodi Smart XL Grill and regulate the settings at Medium for 20 minutes.
2. Mingle the chicken breasts with onion and broccoli in a bowl.
3. Throw in the remaining ingredients and toss thoroughly.
4. Arrange the chicken in the Ninja Foodi when it displays "Add Food".
5. Grill for about 20 minutes, flipping once in between.
6. Dole out in a platter and shower with lemon juice to serve.

Serving Suggestions: Serve over the bed of Basmati rice.

Variation Tip: Adjust the ratio of spices according to your spice tolerance.

Nutritional Information per Serving:

Calories: 352|**Fat:** 14g|**Sat Fat:** 2g|**Carbohydrates:** 5.8g|
Fiber: 0g|**Sugar:** 0.2g|**Protein:** 26g

Delicious Whole Chicken

Preparation Time: 10 minutes
Cooking Time: 25 minutes
Servings: 4

Ingredients:

- 1 teaspoon ground cumin
- ½ tablespoon fresh rosemary, minced
- 1 teaspoon cayenne pepper
- Salt and black pepper, to taste
- 1 tablespoon olive oil
- 1 teaspoon red pepper flakes, crushed
- 1 pound organic whole chicken, neck and giblet removed

Preparation:

1. Select the "Grill" button on the Ninja Foodi Smart XL Grill and regulate the settings at Medium for 25 minutes.
2. Mingle the rosemary, ground cumin, cayenne pepper, red pepper flakes, salt, and black pepper in a bowl.
3. Scrub the chicken with the spice mixture and olive oil.
4. Throw in the remaining ingredients and toss thoroughly.
5. Arrange the chicken in the Ninja Foodi when it displays "Add Food".
6. Grill for about 25 minutes and dole out in a platter.
7. Slice the chicken as you desire and serve.

Serving Suggestions: Serve and enjoy with honey glazed veggies.

Variation Tip: Select the whole chicken with a pinkish hue, which is an indication of fresh meat.

Nutritional Information per Serving:

Calories: 207|**Fat:** 7g|**Sat Fat:** 1.4g|**Carbohydrates:** 1g|
Fiber: 0.5g|**Sugar:** 0.1g|**Protein:** 33.1g

Grilled Chicken Breasts

Preparation Time: 5 minutes
Cooking Time: 15 minutes
Servings: 4

Ingredients:

- ¼ cup red wine vinegar
- 2 tablespoons dijon mustard
- ⅓ cup oil vegetable oil
- 3 tablespoons Worcestershire sauce
- 2 tablespoons lemon juice
- 1 tablespoon salt
- 1 tablespoon sugar
- 4 chicken breasts, boneless skinless
- 2 tablespoons Italian seasoning
- 1 tablespoon black pepper
- 1 teaspoon garlic powder

Preparation:

1. Select the "Grill" button on the Ninja Foodi Smart XL Grill and regulate the settings at Medium for 15 minutes.
2. Mingle all the ingredients in a bowl and scrub the chicken well in this marinade.
3. Arrange the chicken in the Ninja Foodi when it displays "Add Food".
4. Grill for about 15 minutes, flipping once in between.
5. Dole out in a platter and serve warm.

Serving Suggestions: Serve these chicken breasts with grilled vegetables.

Variation Tip: You can also use chicken thighs in this recipe.

Nutritional Information per Serving:

Calories: 238|**Fat:** 14g|**Sat Fat:** 1g|**Carbohydrates:** 2g|
Fiber: 0.1g|**Sugar:** 1g|**Protein:** 24g

Turkey Meatballs

Preparation Time: 15 minutes
Cooking Time: 10 minutes
Servings: 8

Ingredients:

- ½ cup fresh parsley, chopped
- 1 pound extra-lean ground turkey
- 1 cup cooked black beans, mashed roughly
- Olive oil, as required
- 1 yellow bell pepper, seeded and finely chopped
- Salt and black pepper, to taste
- 1 red bell pepper, seeded and finely chopped

Preparation:

1. Select the "Grill" button on the Ninja Foodi Smart XL Grill and regulate the settings at Medium for 10 minutes.
2. Mingle all the ingredients in a bowl and toss well.
3. Form equal sized 24 balls out of this mixture.
4. Arrange the meatballs in the Ninja Foodi when it displays "Add Food".
5. Grill for about 10 minutes, flipping once in between.
6. Dole out in a platter and serve warm.

Serving Suggestions: Serve with balsamic-glazed green beans.

Variation Tip: You can also use green bell peppers.

Nutritional Information per Serving:

Calories: 190|**Fat:** 6.1g|**Sat Fat:** 1.3g|**Carbohydrates:** 17.6g|**Fiber:** 4.2g|**Sugar:** 2g|**Protein:** 17.8g

Thai Chicken

Preparation Time: 10 minutes
Cooking Time: 20 minutes
Servings: 6

Ingredients:

- 2 pounds chicken thighs, skinless
- 1 tablespoon olive oil
- 1 cup tomato salsa, fire-roasted
- 1 teaspoon fresh ginger, finely grated
- ½ cup almond butter
- ¼ teaspoon red pepper flakes, crushed
- 2 tablespoons fresh lime juice
- 1 tablespoon fresh basil, chopped
- 1 tablespoon soy sauce

Preparation:

1. Select the "Grill" button on the Ninja Foodi Smart XL Grill and regulate the settings at Medium for 20 minutes.
2. Mingle chicken thighs with salsa, olive oil, almond butter, lime juice, soy sauce, ginger and red pepper flakes in a bowl and marinate for 3 hours.
3. Arrange the chicken in the Ninja Foodi when it displays "Add Food".
4. Grill for about 20 minutes, flipping once in between.
5. Dole out in a platter and serve garnished with fresh basil.

Serving Suggestions: Enjoy with sautéed vegetables.

Variation Tip: Cashew butter can also be used instead of almond butter.

Nutritional Information per Serving:

Calories: 323|**Fat:** 14.2g|**Sat Fat:** 3.4g|**Carbohydrates:** 2.1g|**Fiber:** 0.3g|**Sugar:** 0.6g|**Protein:** 44.3g

Tex Mex Chicken

Preparation Time: 10 minutes
Cooking Time: 20 minutes
Servings: 6

Ingredients:

- 1 cup tomatoes, chopped finely
- 2 pounds chicken breasts
- 1 cup coconut cream
- ½ teaspoon salt
- 2 tablespoons Mexican seasoning
- 2 tablespoons olive oil
- 1 cup green chilies

Preparation:

1. Select the "Grill" button on the Ninja Foodi Smart XL Grill and regulate the settings at Medium for 20 minutes.
2. Mingle chicken breasts with all other ingredients in a bowl.
3. Arrange the chicken in the Ninja Foodi when it displays "Add Food".
4. Grill for about 20 minutes, flipping once in between.
5. Dole out in a platter and serve warm.

Serving Suggestions: Serve the Tex Mex Chicken with grilled bell peppers.

Variation Tip: Both fresh and frozen meat can be used for this recipe.

Nutritional Information per Serving:

Calories: 323|**Fat:** 14.2g|**Sat Fat:** 3.4g|**Carbohydrates:** 2.1g|
Fiber: 0.3g|**Sugar:** 0.6g|**Protein:** 44.3g

Chapter 6: Beef, Pork & Lamb Recipes

Asparagus Steak Tips

Preparation Time: 5 minutes
Cooking Time: 15 minutes
Servings: 2

Ingredients:

- 1 teaspoon olive oil
- 1 pound steak cubes
- ½ teaspoon salt
- 1/8 teaspoon cayenne pepper
- ½ teaspoon dried onion powder
- ½ teaspoon dried garlic powder
- ½ teaspoon black pepper, freshly ground

CRISPY ASPARAGUS

- 1 pound asparagus, tough ends trimmed
- ¼ teaspoon salt

- ½ teaspoon olive oil

Preparation:

1. Select the "Grill" button on the Ninja Foodi Smart XL Grill and regulate the settings at Medium for 10 minutes.
2. Mingle garlic powder, cayenne pepper, onion powder, salt, and black pepper in a bowl.
3. Shift the steak cubes in a Ziploc bag along with the garlic powder mixture.
4. Arrange the chicken in the Ninja Foodi when it displays "Add Food".
5. Grill for about 10 minutes, tossing the steaks once in between.
6. Dole out in a platter and serve warm.

Serving Suggestions: Fresh baby greens will accompany these Asparagus Steak Tips greatly.

Variation Tip: Don't forget to trim the ends of asparagus.

Nutritional Information per Serving:

Calories: 361|**Fat:** 16.3g|**Sat Fat:** 4.9g|**Carbohydrates:** 9.3g|

Fiber: 0.1g|**Sugar:** 1.3g|**Protein:** 33.3g

Beef Satay

Preparation Time: 5 minutes
Cooking Time: 15 minutes
Servings: 2

Ingredients:

- 1 pound beef flank steak, sliced into long strips
- 2 tablespoons olive oil
- 1 tablespoon fish sauce
- 1 tablespoon sugar
- 1 tablespoon garlic, minced
- ½ cup cilantro, chopped and divided
- 1 tablespoon ginger, minced
- 1 teaspoon ground coriander
- 1 tablespoon soy sauce
- 1 teaspoon Sriracha sauce

Preparation:

1. Select the "Grill" button on the Ninja Foodi Smart XL Grill and regulate the settings at Medium for 15 minutes.
2. Mingle fish sauce with ginger, soy sauce, garlic, coriander, Sriracha, sugar, and ¼ cup cilantro in a bowl.
3. Marinate the beef strips in the fish sauce mixture for about 30 minutes.
4. Arrange the beef strips in the Ninja Foodi when it displays "Add Food" and shower with olive oil.
5. Grill for 15 minutes, flipping once in the middle way.
6. Dish out and serve garnished with cilantro.

Serving Suggestions: Serve this beef satay with 1/4 cup roasted peanuts.

Variation Tip: It is better to marinate it overnight.

Nutritional Information per Serving:

Calories: 695|**Fat:** 17.5g|**Sat Fat:** 4.8g|**Carbohydrates:** 6.4g|
Fiber: 1.8g|**Sugar:** 3.5g|**Protein:** 117.4g

Korean BBQ Beef

Preparation Time: 5 minutes
Cooking Time: 15 minutes
Servings: 2

Ingredients:

FOR THE MEAT:

- Coconut oil spray
- 1 pound Flank steak
- ¼ cup corn starch

FOR THE SAUCE:

- ½ cup soy sauce
- ½ cup brown sugar
- 2 tablespoons Pompeian white wine vinegar
- ½ teaspoon sesame seeds
- 1 clove garlic, crushed
- 1 teaspoon cornstarch
- 1 tablespoon hot chili sauce
- 1 teaspoon water
- 1 teaspoon ground ginger

Preparation:

1. Select the "Grill" button on the Ninja Foodi Smart XL Grill and regulate the settings at Medium for 15 minutes.
2. Grease the grill with the coconut oil spray.
3. Coat the steaks with the corn-starch and transfer into the Ninja Foodi when it shows "Add Food".
4. Mingle rest of the ingredients for the sauce in a pan except corn-starch and water.
5. Whip corn-starch with water in a bowl and add to the sauce.
6. Cook on medium-low heat until it thickens and drizzle the sauce over the steaks to serve.

Serving Suggestions: Enjoy this steak with grilled potatoes.

Variation Tip: Flank steak is best when it's cooked medium-rare.

Nutritional Information per Serving:

Calories: 545|**Fat:** 36.4g|**Sat Fat:** 10.1g|**Carbohydrates:** 0.7g| **Fiber:** 0.2g|**Sugar:** 0.2g|**Protein:** 42.5g

Crispy Pork Belly

Preparation Time: 5 minutes
Cooking Time: 20 minutes
Servings: 4

Ingredients:

- 2 packages pork belly, diced into 1-inch cubes
- ½ cup coconut aminos
- ½ cup coconut vinegar
- Salt, to taste
- Coconut oil spray
- ¼ teaspoon fish sauce
- ¼ cup Sriracha

Preparation:

1. Select the "Air Crisp" button on the Ninja Foodi Smart XL Grill and regulate the settings at Medium for 20 minutes.
2. Mingle pork belly with coconut vinegar, aminos, fish sauce, and Sriracha in a Ziploc bag.
3. Shake the Ziploc bag to coat the pork belly well and marinate for about 4 hours.
4. Scrub the oil and salt on both sides of the pork.
5. Arrange the pork cubes in the Ninja Foodi when it displays "Add Food".
6. Air crisp for the about 20 minutes, flipping once in between.
7. Dole out in a platter and serve warm.

Serving Suggestions: Serve with ketchup or your favorite sauce.

Variation Tip: Pork chops can also be used in this recipe.

Nutritional Information per Serving:

Calories: 301|**Fat:** 15.8g|**Sat Fat:** 2.7g|**Carbohydrates:** 11.7g|
Fiber: 0.3g|**Sugar:** 2.2g|**Protein:** 28.2g

Steak and Mushrooms

Preparation Time: 5 minutes
Cooking Time: 10 minutes
Servings: 4

Ingredients:

- ¼ cup Worcestershire sauce
- 1 pound beef sirloin steak, cubed into 1-inch pieces
- 8-ounces mushrooms, sliced
- 1 teaspoon parsley flakes
- 1 teaspoon chili flakes, crushed
- 1 tablespoon olive oil
- 1 teaspoon paprika

Preparation:

1. Select the "Air Crisp" button on the Ninja Foodi Smart XL Grill and regulate the settings at 400 degrees F for 10 minutes.
2. Scrub the steak with olive oil, mushrooms, parsley, paprika, chili flakes, and Worcestershire sauce in a bowl.
3. Wrap the bowl and marinate in the refrigerator for about 3 hours.
4. Arrange the steaks and mushrooms in the Ninja Foodi when it displays "Add Food".
5. Air crisp for about 10 minutes, tossing once in between.
6. Dole out in a platter and serve warm.

Serving Suggestions: Fig and arugula salad will brighten the taste of tenderloin.

Variation Tip: The addition of dried herbs will add a delish touch in pork tenderloin.

Nutritional Information per Serving:

Calories: 405|**Fat:** 22.7g|**Sat Fat:** 6.1g|**Carbohydrates:** 6.1g|
Fiber: 1.4g|**Sugar:** 2.3g|**Protein:** 45.2g

Memphis-Style Pork Ribs

Preparation Time: 5 minutes
Cooking Time: 20 minutes
Servings: 6

Ingredients:

- 1 teaspoon onion powder
- 2¼ pounds pork spareribs
- 1 tablespoon sweet paprika
- ½ teaspoon mustard powder
- 1 tablespoon kosher salt
- 1 teaspoon garlic powder
- ½ teaspoon black pepper
- 1 tablespoon dark brown sugar
- 1 teaspoon poultry seasoning

Preparation:

1. Select the "Grill" button on the Ninja Foodi Smart XL Grill and regulate the settings at Medium for 20 minutes.
2. Mingle poultry seasoning, salt, sugar, paprika, onion powder, pepper, mustard powder, and garlic powder in a bowl.
3. Shift the the pork ribs in the poultry seasoning mixture and rub well.
4. Arrange the pork ribs in the Ninja Foodi when it displays "Add Food".
5. Grill for about 20 minutes, tossing once in the middle way.
6. Dole out in a platter and serve warm.

Serving Suggestions: Serve these pork ribs with curried potato salad.

Variation Tip: Bring the pork ribs to room temperature before cooking.

Nutritional Information per Serving:

Calories: 452|**Fat:** 4g|**Sat Fat:** 2g|**Carbohydrates:** 23.1g|
Fiber: 0g|**Sugar:** 5.3g|**Protein:** 26g

Herb Crusted Chops

Preparation Time: 5 minutes
Cooking Time: 12 minutes
Servings: 2

Ingredients:

- 1 teaspoon olive oil
- 1 pound pork loin chops bone-in
- 1 tablespoon herb and garlic seasoning

Preparation:

1. Select the "Air Crisp" button on the Ninja Foodi Smart XL Grill and regulate the settings at Medium for 12 minutes.
2. Mingle the steak with olive oil and seasoning mixture in a bowl.
3. Arrange the steaks in the Ninja Foodi when it displays "Add Food".
4. Air crisp for about 12 minutes, flipping once in between.
5. Dole out in a platter and serve warm.

Serving Suggestions: Serve these herb crusted chops with creamed spinach.

Variation Tip: You can also add fresh ginger and garlic to enhance the taste.

Nutritional Information per Serving:

Calories: 609|**Fat:** 50.5g|**Sat Fat:** 11.7g|**Carbohydrates:** 9.9g| **Fiber:** 1.5g|**Sugar:** 1.7g|**Protein:** 29.3g

Beef with Mixed Herb Butter

Preparation Time: 5 minutes
Cooking Time: 20 minutes
Servings: 4

Ingredients:

- 1 lemon, halved
- 4 (6-ounce) beef steaks
- 2 teaspoons fresh dill, chopped
- 2 teaspoons fresh thyme
- Salt and black pepper, to taste
- 2½ tablespoons butter, unsalted
- 2 garlic cloves, minced

Preparation:

1. Select the "Broil" button on the Ninja Foodi Smart XL Grill and regulate the settings for 20 minutes.
2. Dust the beef steaks with thyme, dill, garlic, salt, and black pepper in a bowl.
3. Mingle the dusted steaks with butter and lemon juice.
4. Arrange the beef steaks in the Ninja Foodi when it displays "Add Food".
5. Broil for 20 minutes and dole out in a platter to serve warm.

Serving Suggestions: Baked cauliflower will nicely accompany this beef dish.

Variation Tip: Add in rosemary for enhanced taste.

Nutritional Information per Serving:

Calories: 389|**Fat:** 17.9g|**Sat Fat:** 8.6g|**Carbohydrates:** 2.5g|
Fiber: 0.7g|**Sugar:** 0.4g|**Protein:** 52.1g

Garlic and Rosemary Grilled Lamb Chops

Preparation Time: 15 minutes
Cooking Time: 15 minutes
Servings: 6

Ingredients:

- 4 garlic cloves, minced
- 2 pounds lamb chops, thick cut
- 1 tablespoon fresh rosemary, chopped
- ½ teaspoon ground black pepper
- ¼ cup olive oil
- 1¼ teaspoons salt
- 1 lemon zest

Preparation:

1. Select the "Grill" button on the Ninja Foodi Smart XL Grill and regulate the settings at Medium for 15 minutes.
2. Mingle garlic, rosemary, salt, pepper, lemon zest and olive oil in a bowl.
3. Coat the lamb chops with the garlic mixture and marinate overnight.
4. Arrange the lamb chops in the Ninja Foodi when it displays "Add Food".
5. Grill for about 15 minutes, flipping once in between.
6. Dole out in a platter and serve warm.

Serving Suggestions: Serve the lamb chops with mashed potatoes or polenta.

Variation Tip: Remember to pat dry the lamb chops before seasoning.

Nutritional Information per Serving:

Calories: 290|**Fat:** 14.2g|**Sat Fat:** 4.7g|**Carbohydrates:** 20.3g|
Fiber: 6.8g|**Sugar:** 4.1g|**Protein:** 21.2g

Beef Sirloin Steak

Preparation Time: 10 minutes
Cooking Time: 30 minutes
Servings: 6

Ingredients:

- 1 teaspoon garlic powder
- 2 pounds beef top sirloin steaks
- 2 garlic cloves, minced
- Salt and black pepper, to taste
- ¼ cup olive oil

Preparation:

1. Select the "Grill" button on the Ninja Foodi Smart XL Grill and regulate the settings at Medium for 15 minutes.
2. Mingle beef sirloin steaks with all other ingredients in a bowl.
3. Arrange the beef sirloin steaks in the Ninja Foodi when it displays "Add Food".
4. Grill for about 15 minutes, flipping once in between.
5. Dole out in a platter and serve warm.

Serving Suggestions: Serve with a baked potato.

Variation Tip: Butter can also be used instead of olive oil.

Nutritional Information per Serving:

Calories: 246|**Fat:** 13.1g|**Sat Fat:** 7.6g|**Carbohydrates:** 2g|
Fiber: 0.1g|**Sugar:** 0.1g|**Protein:** 31.3g

Beef Stroganoff

Preparation Time: 10 minutes
Cooking Time: 20 minutes
Servings: 3

Ingredients:

- ½ cup onions, diced
- 1 tablespoon olive oil
- ¾ cup water
- ½ cup sour cream
- 1 tablespoon garlic
- 1½ cups mushroom, chopped

- 1 teaspoon black pepper
- 1 pound beef stew meat
- 1 teaspoon salt
- 1 teaspoon salt

Preparation:

1. Select the "Bake" button on the Ninja Foodi Smart XL Grill and regulate the settings at 350 degrees F for 15 minutes.
2. Sauté garlic and onions in the olive oil in a pan for 3 minutes.
3. Mingle beef with sautéed garlic and onions in a bowl.
4. Stir in rest of the ingredients except sour cream and toss well.
5. Arrange the beef mixture in the Ninja Foodi when it displays "Add Food".
6. Bake for about 15 minutes, tossing once in between.
7. Whip in the avocado cream and bake for 2 more minutes.
8. Dole out in a bowl and serve hot.

Serving Suggestions: Roasted asparagus will be great if served with Beef Stroganoff.

Variation Tip: You can also use avocado cream instead of sour cream.

Nutritional Information per Serving:

Calories: 406|**Fat:** 19.8g|**Sat Fat:** 4.9g|**Carbohydrates:** 7.6g|**Fiber:** 3.6g|**Sugar:** 1.6g|**Protein:** 48.2g

Country Steak

Preparation Time: 10 minutes
Cooking Time: 20 minutes
Servings: 6

Ingredients:

- 4 garlic cloves, minced
- 1½ tablespoons canola oil
- ½ teaspoon black pepper
- 2 pounds beef round steaks
- ½ cup almond flour
- ½ cup onions, diced
- ½ cup ketchup
- 2 teaspoons Worcestershire sauce
- ¾ teaspoon salt

Preparation:

1. Select the "Grill" button on the Ninja Foodi Smart XL Grill and regulate the settings at Medium for 20 minutes.
2. Coat both sides of the beef steaks with flour and add the remaining ingredients.
3. Arrange the beef steaks mixture in the Ninja Foodi when it displays "Add Food".
4. Grill for about 20 minutes, flipping once in between.
5. Dole out in a platter and serve hot.

Serving Suggestions: Mashed cauliflower makes a classic pairing with Country Steaks.

Variation Tip: Almond flour can be replaced with all-purpose flour.

Nutritional Information per Serving:

Calories: 472|**Fat:** 26.6g|**Sat Fat:** 6.6g|**Carbohydrates:** 8g|
Fiber: 0.8g|**Sugar:** 5.3g|**Protein:** 49g

Chapter 7: Dessert Recipes

Grilled Pineapple Sundaes

Preparation Time: 10 minutes
Cooking Time: 4 minutes
Servings: 4

Ingredients:

- 2 tablespoons sweetened coconut, toasted and shredded
- 4 scoops vanilla ice cream
- 4 pineapple slices
- Dulce de leche, for drizzling

Preparation:

1. Select the "Grill" button on the Ninja Foodi Smart XL Grill and regulate the settings at Medium for 4 minutes.
2. Arrange the pineapple slices in the Ninja Foodi when it displays "Add Food".
3. Grill for about 4 minutes, turning once in between.
4. Dole out in a plate when completely grilled.
5. Place the scoops of vanilla ice cream over the grilled pineapple slices.
6. Trickle Dulce de leche and shredded coconut over the pineapples to serve.

Serving Suggestions: You can serve it with a waffle.

Variation Tip: Caramel ice cream scoop can replace the vanilla flavor.

Nutritional Information per Serving:

Calories: 338|**Fat:** 9.5g|**Sat Fat:** 6.3g|**Carbohydrates:** 61g|
Fiber: 3g|**Sugar:** 46.2g|**Protein:** 5.3g

Blooming Grilled Apples

Preparation Time: 10 minutes
Cooking Time: 30 minutes
Servings: 4

Ingredients:

- 8 tablespoons maple cream caramel sauce, divided
- 4 small baking apples
- 12 teaspoons chopped pecans, divided

Preparation:

1. Select the "Grill" button on the Ninja Foodi Smart XL Grill and regulate the settings for 30 minutes.
2. Trim the upper part of the apples and scoop out the cores of the apples.
3. Chop the apple around the center and insert fine cuts surrounding the apple.
4. Shove the pecans and maple cream caramel sauce in the middle of the apple.
5. Cover the apple with the foil and arrange the apple inside the Ninja Foodi when it displays "Add Food".
6. Dole out in a platter and to serve immediately.

Serving Suggestions: Serve with 4 scoops of vanilla ice cream.

Variation Tip: Choose firm apples.

Nutritional Information per Serving:

Calories: 407|**Fat:** 23g|**Sat Fat:** 12g|**Carbohydrates:** 50g|
Fiber: 50g|**Sugar:** 32.4g|**Protein:** 4g

S'mores Roll-Up

Preparation Time: 10 minutes
Cooking Time: 5 minutes
Servings: 2

Ingredients:

- 4 graham crackers
- 2 cups mini marshmallows
- 2 flour tortillas
- 2 cups chocolate chips

Preparation:

1. Select the "Grill" button on the Ninja Foodi Smart XL Grill and regulate the settings at Medium for 5 minutes.
2. Split the graham crackers, chocolate chips, and marshmallows on the tortillas.
3. Tightly wrap up the tortillas and arrange them inside the Ninja Foodi when it displays "Add Food".
4. Grill for 5 minutes, flipping once in between.
5. Dole out in a plate when completely grilled to serve.

Serving Suggestions: Topping of chopped nuts will add a nice nutty texture.

Variation Tip: You can also use white chocolate chips.

Nutritional Information per Serving:

Calories: 429|**Fat:** 13.6g|**Sat Fat:** 6g|**Carbohydrates:** 72.7g| **Fiber:** 3.3g|**Sugar:** 57.8g|**Protein:** 5.9g

Chocolate Marshmallow Banana

Preparation Time: 10 minutes
Cooking Time: 5 minutes
Servings: 2

Ingredients:

- 2 bananas, peeled
- 1 cup chocolate chips
- 1 cup mini marshmallows

Preparation:

1. Select the "Grill" button on the Ninja Foodi Smart XL Grill and regulate the settings at Medium for 5 minutes.
2. Arrange the banana on a foil paper and cut it lengthwise, leaving behind the ends.
3. Insert the chocolate chips and marshmallows in the bananas and tightly wrap the foil.
4. Arrange the filled bananas inside the Ninja Foodi when it displays "Add Food".
5. Dole out in a platter and unwrap to serve and enjoy.

Serving Suggestions: Serve with extra grilled marshmallows on skewers.

Variation Tip: Make sure to use fresh bananas.

Nutritional Information per Serving:

Calories: 137|**Fat:** 1g|**Sat Fat:** 0.6g|**Carbohydrates:** 33.3g|
Fiber: 3.3g|**Sugar:** 12g|**Protein:** 1.6g

Grilled Donut Ice Cream Sandwich

Preparation Time: 10 minutes
Cooking Time: 3 minutes
Servings: 4

Ingredients:

- 4 glazed donuts, cut in half
- 8 scoops vanilla ice cream
- 1 cup cream, whipped
- 4 cherries, maraschino

Preparation:

1. Select the "Grill" button on the Ninja Foodi Smart XL Grill and regulate the settings at Medium for 3 minutes.
2. Arrange the donut halves, glazed side down in the Ninja Foodi when it displays "Add Food".
3. Dole out in a platter and stuff vanilla ice cream inside each donut sandwich.
4. Top with whipped cream and cherry to serve.

Serving Suggestions: Serve with the drizzling of chocolate syrup.

Variation Tip: Strawberry ice cream can be used if you want to change the flavor.

Nutritional Information per Serving:

Calories: 558|**Fat:** 27.5g|**Sat Fat:** 13.2g|**Carbohydrates:** 70.9g|
Fiber: 2.5g|**Sugar:** 28.4g|**Protein:** 7.5g

Grilled Fruit Skewers

Preparation Time: 20 minutes
Cooking Time: 12 minutes
Servings: 12

Ingredients:

- 8 peaches, sliced
- 1½ pints strawberries, sliced
- 1½ cups pineapples, cut into large cubes
- 3 tablespoons honey
- Salt, to taste
- 3 tablespoons olive oil
- 10 skewers, soaked in water for 20 minutes

Preparation:

1. Select the "Grill" button on the Ninja Foodi Smart XL Grill and regulate the settings at Medium for 12 minutes.
2. Insert the strawberries, pineapples, and peaches on the skewers.
3. Dust with salt and shower with olive oil.
4. Arrange the skewers inside the Ninja Foodi when it displays "Add Food".
5. Grill for 12 minutes, turning twice in between.
6. Trickle the grilled fruits with honey and serve well.

Serving Suggestions: Serve with whipped cream.

Variation Tip: Measure the ingredients with care.

Nutritional Information per Serving:

Calories: 132|**Fat:** 4.7g|**Sat Fat:** 0.6g|**Carbohydrates:** 23.8g| **Fiber:** 3.3g|**Sugar:** 21.4g|**Protein:** 1.6g

Chocolate Peanut Butter Cups

Preparation Time: 10 minutes
Cooking Time: 31 minutes
Servings: 3

Ingredients:

- ¼ cup heavy cream
- 1 cup butter
- 2 ounces unsweetened chocolate
- 4 packets stevia
- ¼ cup peanut butter, separated

Preparation:

1. Select the "Bake" button on the Ninja Foodi Smart XL Grill and regulate the settings at 360 degrees F for 30 minutes.
2. Microwave the peanut butter and butter for 1 minute in a bowl.
3. Mingle in the unsweetened chocolate, stevia, and heavy cream.
4. Pour the peanut butter mixture in a baking mold.
5. Arrange the baking mold inside the Ninja Foodi when it displays "Add Food".
6. Bake for 30 minutes, turning twice in between.
7. Trickle the grilled fruits with honey and serve.

Serving Suggestions: Sprinkle the peanut butter cups with powdered sugar before serving.

Variation Tip: Use the best quality peanut butter.

Nutritional Information per Serving:

Calories: 479|**Fat:** 51.5g|**Sat Fat:** 29.7g|**Carbohydrates:** 7.7g|**Fiber:** 2.7g|**Sugar:** 1.4g|**Protein:** 5.2g

Cream Crepes

Preparation Time: 10 minutes
Cooking Time: 16 minutes
Servings: 6

Ingredients:

- 3 organic eggs
- 1½ teaspoons Splenda
- 3 tablespoons coconut flour
- 3 tablespoons coconut oil, melted and divided
- ½ cup heavy cream

Preparation:

1. Select the "Grill" button on the Ninja Foodi Smart XL Grill and regulate the settings at Medium for 12 minutes.
2. Mingle together 1½ tablespoons of coconut oil, Splenda, eggs and salt in a bowl.
3. Slowly fold in the coconut flour and heavy cream.
4. Pour about ¼ of the mixture inside the Ninja Foodi when it displays "Add Food".
5. Grill for 5 minutes, flipping once in between.
6. Repeat with the remaining mixture in batches and serve.

Serving Suggestions: Fresh strawberries will go great with cream crepes.

Variation Tip: Almond flour can also be used.

Nutritional Information per Serving:

Calories: 145|**Fat:** 13.1g|**Sat Fat:** 9.1g|**Carbohydrates:** 4g|
Fiber: 1.5g|**Sugar:** 1.2g|**Protein:** 3.5g

Fudge Divine

Preparation Time: 20 minutes
Cooking Time: 14 minutes
Servings: 24

Ingredients:

- 1 cup heavy whipping cream
- ½ teaspoon organic vanilla extract
- 2-ounce butter, softened
- 2-ounce 70% dark chocolate, finely chopped

Preparation:

1. Select the "Bake" button on the Ninja Foodi Smart XL Grill and regulate the settings at 360 degrees F for 14 minutes.
2. Mingle cream with vanilla, butter, and chocolate in a bowl.
3. Pour the cream mixture in a baking mold.
4. Arrange the baking mold inside the Ninja Foodi when it displays "Add Food".
5. Bake for 14 minutes and dole out in a dish.
6. Refrigerate it for few hours and serve chilled.

Serving Suggestions: Serve with fresh cream.

Variation Tip: You can also make it with other chocolates.

Nutritional Information per Serving:

Calories: 292|**Fat:** 26.2g|**Sat Fat:** 16.3g|**Carbohydrates:** 8.2g|
Fiber: 0g|**Sugar:** 6.6g|**Protein:** 5.2g

Conclusion

In the end, without a doubt, the Ninja Foodi Smart XL Grill is the most suitable, as well as the best available single Smart device that can replace almost all the other conventional cooking appliances in your kitchen. It is going to serve as a multi-tasking cooking device that is going to perform air crisping, simmering, searing, sautéing, pressure cooking, broiling, slow cooking, dehydration, and much more with a single touch of a button. The Smart built-in programs are going to make the device more reliable and convenient for users than any of its competitors.

There is almost nothing hard in understanding or mastering the Ninja Foodi Smart XL Grill at all. You don't have to do any significant hard work in learning the device and providing yourself and your loved ones with the best aroma, nutritious food, and finger-licking taste. It is the most convenient cooking device to use, and even the cleaning process is not that hard at all too. It can be thoroughly and easily cleaned inside a dishwasher apart from the central unit. Keep in mind that the main unit should not and cannot be soaked or immersed in any sort of liquid whatsoever for cleaning purposes.

Made in the USA
Monee, IL
14 December 2020